Armchair Golf:
Observations on
Our Favorite Pastime

Edited by Alison Bing

BARNES
& NOBLE
BOOKS

NEW YORK

The quotes in this book have been drawn from many sources, and are assumed to be accurate as quoted in their previously published forms. Although every effort has been made to verify the quotes and sources, the publisher cannot guarantee their perfect accuracy.

2003 Barnes & Noble Books

ISBN 0-7607-4065-8

Printed and bound in the United States of America

M 9 8 7 6 5 4 3 2

GREETINGS, GOLFERS—

Here are a few choice words for you. No, not the kind you might hear in the rough or after a short putt gone awry—those aren't to be repeated in polite company, or at least around non-golfers who fail to appreciate the agony of the triple-bogey.

These words are chosen by great golfers, commentators, and thinkers to describe the highs, lows, and many-contorted positions of any golf game. This is the game not as you learn it from the club-house instructor or see it on TV, but as it's actually played—when you forget most things you've been taught, trust your body to remember, and discover the improbable joy of hitting a drive straight and true—only to watch it land in the sand trap.

You know the feeling…and with a few judiciously applied quotes from this book, so will those benighted few in your life who can't yet relate to the glories of the green. Wax philosophical about a bad shot with an observation by the likes of Lee Trevino or Babe Didrikson Zaharias, and you're bound to win your golfing partners' respect, if not their money. Even if you can't swing like Tiger Woods or sink a putt like Annika Sorenstam, you can still wisecrack with the best of them at the nineteenth hole.

May your score be diminutive, your handicap formidable, and your choice of quotes just right.

—ALISON BING
(who has never looked back since her first glorious days
on the links at age seven—which is probably
how she wound up backing up over her
grandfather with the golf cart)

The Name
of the Game

It was named golf because all of the other four-letter words were already taken.

—RAYMOND FLOYD

Have you ever noticed what golf spells backwards?

—AL BOLISKA

If you watch a game, it's fun. If you play it, it's recreation. If you work at it, it's golf.

—BOB HOPE

Golf is a game in which a ball—one and a half inches in diameter—is placed on another ball—8,000 miles in diameter. The object being: To hit the small ball, but not the larger.

—John Cunningham

Golf is a game whose aim is to hit a very small ball into an even smaller hole, with weapons singularly ill-designed for the purpose.

—Winston Churchill

Golf and sex are the only things you can enjoy without being good at them.

—Jimmy Demaret

The biggest liar in the world is the golfer who claims he plays the game merely for exercise.

—Tommy Bolt

People who say golf is fun are probably the same people who rationalize the game by saying they play it for their health. What could be fun about a game in the entire history of which nobody has ever shot the score he thought he should have?

—CHARLES PRICE

Golf is 90 percent inspiration and 10 percent perspiration.

—JOHNNY MILLER

Golf: A good walk spoiled.

—MARK TWAIN

Golf: A good cart ride spoiled.

—BERNIE LINCICOME

Golf is not just exercise; it is an adventure, a romance...a Shakespeare play in which disaster and comedy are intertwined [and] you have to live with the consequences of each action.

—HAROLD SEGALL

Golf is a day spent in strenuous idleness.

—WILLIAM WORDSWORTH

Golf is twenty percent mechanics and technique. The other eighty percent is philosophy, humor, tragedy, romance, melodrama, companionship, camaraderie, cussedness, and conversation.

—GRANTLAND RICE

My psychiatrist prescribed a game of golf as an antidote to the feelings of euphoria I experience from time to time.

—BRUCE LANSKY

It is almost impossible to remember how tragic a place the world is when one is playing golf.

—Robert Lynd

All games are silly, but golf, if you look at it dispassionately, goes to extremes.

—Peter Aliss

Golf is, in part, a game; but only in part. It is also in part a religion, a fever, a vice, a mirage, a frenzy, a fear, an abscess, a joy, a thrill, a pest, a disease, an uplift, a brooding, a melancholy, a dream of yesterday, and a hope for tomorrow.

—New York Tribune, 1916

They say golf is like life, but don't believe them. Golf is more complicated than that.

—Gardner Dickinson

Getting
Geared Up

You can't go into a shop and buy a good game of golf.

—SAM SNEAD

[Since the early days of golf] rocket science moved into the picture. Golf clubs and balls are made of exotic metals, fissionable materials. You could either shoot par or bomb Paris with them.

—JIM MURRAY

The game of golf would lose a good deal if croquet mallets and billiard cues were allowed on the putting green.

—ERNEST HEMINGWAY, in a 1925 letter

Golf: A game in which you claim the privileges of age, and retain the playthings of childhood.

—SAMUEL JOHNSON

Golf is tiddlywinks played while standing up and wearing a hat.

—FLORENCE KING

The reason most people play golf is to wear clothes they would not be caught dead in otherwise.

—ROGER SIMON

Golf is…caught in some 1970s fashion time warp of Pringles sweaters and hideous tartan trousers made of Crimplene, a substance long abandoned in every other sphere of human existence. Golf is acknowledged for the breeding of truly hellish haircuts, bleary gin-and-tonic politics and obsessive collectors of monogrammed tees. So why do I love it so?

—TOM MORTON, *Hell's Golfer: A Good Walk Spoiled*

———※———

"Play it as it lies" is one of the fundamental dictates of golf. The other is "Wear it if it clashes."

—HENRY BEARD

———※———

I always keep a supply of stimulants handy in case I see a snake, which I also keep handy.

—W. C. FIELDS, explaining the whiskey flask in his golf bag

A Little Friendly Competition

Every rock 'n' roll band I know, guys with long hair and tattoos, plays golf now.

—Alice Cooper

The only way of really finding out a man's true character is to play golf with him. In no other walk of life does the cloven hoof so quickly display itself.

—P. G. Wodehouse

The uglier the man's legs are, the better he plays golf. It's almost a law.

–H. G. Wells

<hr>

So Agatha spoke about golf and about the love men have for one another. "It's the only reason ye play at all," she said. "...All the waitin' and oohin' and ahin' o'er yer shots, all the talk o' this one's drive and that one's putt and the other one's gorgeous swing—what is it all but love? Men lovin' men, that's what golf is."

–Michael Murphy, *Golf in the Kingdom*

<hr>

I play [golf] with friends sometimes, but there are never friendly games.

–Ben Hogan

<hr>

Never bet with anyone you meet on the first tee who has a deep suntan, a one iron in his bag and squinty eyes.

–Dave Marr

How would you like to meet the top 143 people at what you do each week in order to survive?

—BRUCE CRAMPTON

———⊙———

This is how you really find out if you have the nerves to handle the pressure.

—Tennis champion BILLIE JEAN KING,
on 11-time LPGA champion Annika Sorenstam's
decision to play in a men's PGA event at the
7,080-yard Colonial course in May, 2003

———⊙———

Golf is a game of coordination, rhythm and grace; women have these to a high degree.

—BABE DIDRIKSON ZAHARIAS

———⊙———

Of course, if golf establishment types had their way all the time, Tiger Woods would be a caddie, Karrie Webb would be schlepping drinks at the 19th hole, and...Casey Martin would have never been allowed near a golf course in the first place. Golf, because of silly little things like the law and equal rights, hides its snobbery and prejudice these days. But they're still there.

—MARK MADDEN, on the flap over disabled golfer Casey Martin's 2001 ADA appeal to the USGA to be allowed to use a cart

Although golf was originally restricted to wealthy, overweight Protestants, today it's open to anybody who owns hideous clothing.

—DAVE BARRY

I never thought guys like Lee [Elder] and Jim [Dent] would make it as long as they did, because they never had a chance growing up to play against the best, nor did they play the best golf courses. Once they did make it, they still didn't have the sponsorship money. Even the young (minority) professionals don't realize the struggles that went on in breaking those barriers. It's a tough thing to try to explain to them, but everybody needs to remember. Those were some difficult times for a lot of good people who really loved the game.

—NORRIS HORTON,
former United Golf Association President

⸺◈⸺

If every golfer in the world, male and female, were laid end to end, I for one would leave them there.

—MICHAEL PARKINSON

⸺◈⸺

Greens Fees
and Other Forms of Larceny

I regard golf as an expensive way of playing marbles.

—G. K. CHESTERTON

If there is any larceny in a man, golf will bring it out.

—PAUL GALLICO

To be truthful, I think golfers are overpaid. It's unreal, and I have trouble dealing with the guilt sometimes.

—COLIN MONTGOMERIE

If Horatio Alger Jr. were alive today, he would love to write the tale of Jose Coceres, from Argentina rags to golf riches. The 38-year-old 140-pounder just won his second PGA Tour event, raising his 2001 take to $1.49 mil. Not bad for a poor ragged kid who learned to swing with a tree limb and subsequently helped raise 10 impoverished siblings.

—Blackie Sherrod

⎯⎯⎯ ⦿ ⎯⎯⎯

Golf is typical capitalist lunacy.

—George Bernard Shaw

⎯⎯⎯ ⦿ ⎯⎯⎯

It's All a Matter
of Course

Competitive golf is played mainly on a five-and-a-
half-inch course: the space between your ears.

—BOBBY JONES

The vital thing about a hole is that it should either
be more difficult than it looks or look more difficult than it is. It must never be what it looks.

—SIR WALTER SIMPSON

Success depends almost entirely on how effectively you learn to manage the game's two ultimate adversaries: the course and yourself.

—JACK NICKLAUS

<hr>

The golfer plays against the course, and if it all goes wrong, only the golfer is to blame. Problems in golf are due the time it takes the golfer between shots to walk to the ball, probably worrying if the previous shot was not too good and if the process is about to be repeated. The point is made that in other sports, such as tennis and football, the ball comes to you and you react instinctively with little time to think, and therefore under less mental pressure.

—PETER ALLIS, *Easier Golf*

<hr>

If you try to fight the course, it will beat you.

—LOU GRAHAM

<hr>

A good golf course makes you want to play so badly you hardly have time to change your shoes.

—Ben Crenshaw

⸻⸻⸻◉⸻⸻⸻

People who want to play golf on courses straddling three countries are just mentally deranged.

—Pong Leng-ee, former Chief of Thailand's Forestry Department, on a new golf course proposed by a Burmese general that would feature fairways and greens on landmine-filled territory in Burma, Cambodia, and Thailand

⸻⸻⸻◉⸻⸻⸻

Augusta National is like playing a Salvador Dali landscape. I expected a clock to fall out of the trees and hit me in the face.

—David Feherty

⸻⸻⸻◉⸻⸻⸻

It's more than just a little wet. It's a quagmire out there right now. Pretty muddy. We saw one spectator eat it. So it's going to be amazing to see if they can actually get this course playable so we don't have to play lift, clean, and cheat.

—TIGER WOODS,
on the 2002 Championship Tour in Atlanta, Georgia

When I'm on a golf course and it starts to rain and lightning, I hold up my one iron, 'cause I know even God can't hit a one iron.

—LEE TREVINO

[On televised golf matches,] occasionally you hear piano music in the background. Now, where the hell is the piano? Where I play, on ratty public courses, it's more like Dr. Dre on a boom box.

—BILL GEIST,
Fore!Play: The Last American Male Takes up Golf

There's something I call the 'television effect.' Golfers watch the U.S. National Tournament at the Augusta [Georgia] golf course, one of the world's great courses. The course has been styled to appear perfect for a TV show, although it doesn't look that good for the rest of the year. But golfers around the country see that magnificent-looking course, and then pressure their local golf course managers to replicate the Augusta course even though the local climate, soils, and native plants may not be at all like those in the Southeast.

—MICHAEL ALEXANDER,
chair of the Sierra Club's Presidio Task Force

Caddy Wisdom

When he gets the ball into a tough place, that's when he's most relaxed. I think it's because he has so much experience at it.

—DON CHRISTOPHER, Jack Lemmon's caddie

My caddie told me he was getting blisters from raking so much.

—JOANNE CARNER,
on her caddy's subtle hint to stay out of the bunkers

[Caddies] can give you lines off the tee, they can give you lines on the green, they can club you within a few holes of seeing your swing…and whatever your abilities, they can give advice on the shot required. More importantly, a good caddie is also a companion. He can tell you the worst pubs to drink in.

—RICHARD MACKENZIE, *A Wee Nip at the 19th Hole*

Caddies are a breed of their own. If you shoot a 66, they'll say, "Man, we shot a 66!" But go and shoot 77 and they'll say, "Man, he shot a 77!"

—LEE TREVINO

Show up, keep up, and shut up.

—BRUCE SUMMERHAYS, Senior PGA Tour golfer, relaying instructions he received before caddying for his daughter at the U.S. Women's Open

I jump ship in Hong Kong and make my way over to Tibet, and I get on as a looper at a course over in the Himalayas. A looper, you know, a caddy, a looper, a jock. So, I tell them I'm a pro jock, and who do you think they give me? The Dalai Lama, himself... So we finish the eighteenth and he's gonna stiff me. And I say, "Hey, Lama, hey, how about a little something, you know, for the effort, you know." And he says, "Oh, uh, there won't be any money, but when you die, on your deathbed, you will receive total consciousness." So I got that goin' for me, which is nice.

—Carl Spackler (Bill Murray), in *Caddyshack*

Concentration

It's a lot easier to think about birdies when you don't have to think about diapers.

> —JULI INKSTER, upon winning the 1999 Women's Open at age 38 as a mother of two

You can observe a lot by watching.

> —YOGI BERRA

Let the nothingness into yer shots.

> —MICHAEL MURPHY, *Golf in the Kingdom*

I go into the locker room and find a corner and just sit there. I try to achieve a peaceful state of nothingness that will carry over onto the golf course. If I can get that feeling of quiet and obliviousness within myself, I feel I can't lose.

—JANE BLALOCK

The secret of concentration is the secret of self-discovery. You reach inside yourself to discover your personal resources, and what it takes to match them to the challenge.

—ARNOLD PALMER

I visualize hitting the ball as far as JoAnne Carner, putting like Amy Alcott, looking like Jan Stephenson, and having Carol Mann's husband.

—DINAH SHORE

Well, they're Southern people, and if they know you are working at home they think nothing of walking right in for coffee. But they wouldn't dream of interrupting you at golf.

—HARPER LEE, on why she has done her best creative thinking while playing golf

Golf is very much like a love affair: If you don't take it seriously, it's no fun; if you do, it breaks your heart. Don't break your heart, but flirt with the possibility.

—LOUISE SUGGS

Practice Makes What, Exactly?

They say, "Practice makes perfect." Of course, it doesn't. For the vast majority of golfers, it merely consolidates imperfection.

—HENRY LONGHURST

It's funny, but the more I practice, the luckier I become.

—GARY PLAYER

Through years of experience I have found that air offers less resistance than dirt.

—JACK NICKLAUS, on why he tees his ball high

———— ((●)) ————

Swinging at daisies is like playing electric guitar with a tennis racket: if it were that easy, we could all be Jerry Garcia. The ball changes everything.

—MICHAEL BAMBERGER

———— ((●)) ————

You've just got one problem. You stand too close to the ball after you've hit it.

—SAM SNEAD

———— ((●)) ————

Golf is a simple game which only golfers make difficult.

—PERCY ALLIS, in *Easier Golf*

———— ((●)) ————

The click of a solid wood shot soaring far down the fairway is well worth all the hours of practice.

—Jimmy Demaret

———⊙———

I build confidence when I practice a variety of shots—hitting it high or low, working the ball. A lot of golfers go to the range and just hit full shots. That doesn't build on-course confidence, because you won't always hit full shots out there. My confidence is built on knowing I can effectively work the ball in any circumstance.

—JoAnne Carner

———⊙———

You can talk strategy all you want, but what really matters is resiliency.

—Hale Irwin

———⊙———

The reason the golf pro tells you to keep your head down is so you can't see him laughing.

—PHYLLIS DILLER

That Thing You're Supposed To Keep Your Eyes On

If you think it's hard to meet new people, try picking up the wrong golf ball.

—JACK LEMMON

One of the advantages bowling has over golf is that you very seldom lose a bowling ball.

—DON CARTER, pro bowler

That little ball won't move until you hit it, and there's nothing you can do for it after it has gone.

—BABE DIDRIKSON ZAHARIAS

And the wind shall say "Here were decent
    godless people;
Their only monument the asphalt road
And a thousand lost golf balls."

—T. S. ELIOT, "The Rock, pt. 1"

The Swing,

a.k.a. The Reason You Need To Replace Your Divots

Papa, trust your swing.

> —Note written by ten year old QASS SINGH
> pinned to Vijay Singh's golf bag during the
> 2000 U.S. Masters (which Singh won)

It's not just enough to swing at the ball. You've got to loosen your girdle and really let the ball have it.

> —BABE DIDRIKSON ZAHARIAS,
> when asked how she hits 250 yard drives

How does he know? He doesn't have any.

—NANCY LOPEZ'S response to CBS golf analyst
Ben Wright's comment that women have
a hard time keeping their left arms straight
when they swing because "their boobs
get in the way"

The mashie and its stout brother, the niblick, call for a swing which is rather different from the others, and the putter is a thing apart, but for all shots from the tee and through the green until we take the mashie for pitching up to the hole, the swings are—or should be—identical in their main principles.

—HARRY VARDON, *The Gist of Golf*, 1900

The golf swing is like a suitcase into which we are trying to pack one too many things.

—JOHN UPDIKE

There is one essential only in the golf swing: The ball must be hit.

—Sir Walter Simpson

———⊙———

My golf swing is like ironing a shirt. You get one side smoothed out, turn it over and there is a big wrinkle on the other side. You iron that side, turn it over and there's another wrinkle.

—Tom Watson

———⊙———

The golf swing is like sex. You can't be thinking about the mechanics of the act while you are performing.

—Dave Hill

———⊙———

No one who ever had lessons would have a swing like mine.

—Lee Trevino

———⊙———

The only thing you should force in a golf swing is the club back into the bag.

—Byron Nelson

Holes in One

If I ever make a hole in one,
A thrill that I've never known,
I won't be believed and I'll have no fun,
For I'm sure to be playing alone.

—RICHARD ARMOUR, *Golf is a Four-Letter Word*

The funny thing is, I didn't think I hit it very well.

—101-year-old golfer HAROLD STILSON,
who used a 4-iron to ace a 108-yard hole

Fore!

Afore ye!
> —JOHN KNOX, in the first known instance of
> this warning shouted as a golf ball flew
> toward other players, circa 1770

As if we don't have enough violence on television.
> —BARBARA BUSH, after her husband George
> accidentally hit two spectators with golf balls
> during a 1995 celebrity golf tournament

I know I am getting better at golf because I'm
hitting fewer spectators.
> —GERALD FORD

Golf is a game in which you yell "fore," shoot six, and write down five.

—Paul Harvey

———≈◈≈———

Excuses,
Excuses

Because of the suit I was wearing, I couldn't make a good pivot on the swing.

> —ALAN SHEPARD, astronaut and amateur golfer, talking about his 1971 Apollo 14 lunar golf game

I can't swing the way I want to with four sweaters and my pajamas and a rain jacket on.

> —LEE TREVINO, on playing in Scotland

As of this writing, there are approximately 2,450 reasons why a person hits a rotten shot, and more are being discovered every day.

—Jay Cronley

A competitor will find a way to win. Competitors take bad breaks and use them to drive themselves just that much harder. Quitters take bad breaks and use them as reasons to give up.

—Nancy Lopez

While bombs are falling, players may take cover without penalty for ceasing play… A player whose stroke is affected by the simultaneous explosion of a bomb may play another ball from the same place. Penalty, one stroke.

—Temporary World War II rule at the Richmond Golf Club outside London

Roughing It

I'll take the 2-stroke penalty, but I'll be damned if
I play it where it lies.
—GOLFER ELAINE JOHNSON,
after her shot ricocheted off a tree into her bra

―――――

Golf is a game of endless predicaments.
—CHI CHI RODRIGUEZ

―――――

My goal this year is basically to find the fairways.
—LAURI PETERSON

―――――

The entire handbook can be reduced to three rules. One: You do not touch your ball from the moment you tee it up to the moment you pick it out of the hole. Two: don't bend over when you are in the rough. Three: When you are in the woods, keep clapping your hands.

—CHARLES PRICE

Dams and lakes are sacrificial waters where you make a steady gift of your pride and high-priced balls.

—TOMMY BOLT

INTERVIEWER: What was the trouble on 16?
TIGER WOODS: Probably that the ball ended up in the water.

—At the 2002 World Golf Championships: NEC Invitational

I'd like to see the fairways more narrow. Then everybody would have to play from the rough, not just me.

—Severiano Ballesteros

I'm hitting the woods just great, but I'm having a terrible time getting out of them.

—Harry Toscano

Great Shots

What other people may find in poetry or art museums, I find in the flight of a good drive.

—ARNOLD PALMER

Any time a golfer hits a ball perfectly straight with a big club it is, in my view, a fluke.

—JACK NICKLAUS

Good golf is easier to play—and far more pleasant—than bad golf.

—BABE DIDRIKSON ZAHARIAS

If I had cleared the trees and drove the green, it would've been a great shot.

—Sam Snead

———— ◉ ————

Golf is not a game of great shots. It's a game of the most accurate misses.

—Gene Littler

———— ◉ ————

My favorite shots are the practice swing and the conceded putt. The rest can never be mastered.

—Lord Robertson

———— ◉ ————

He's hit it fat... It will probably be short... It just hit the front edge of the green... It's got no chance... It's rolling but it will stop... It's rolling toward the cup... Well, I'll be damned!

—Jimmy Demaret, on Lew Worsham's winning wedge shot for the 1953 World Championship

———— ◉ ————

Sand Trapped

I stayed in the bunker until I made one.
They had to bring me cocktails and dinner.

—JoAnne Carner, on how she learned
to chip her way out of sand traps

The object of a bunker or trap is not only to punish a physical mistake, to punish lack of control,
but also to punish pride and egotism.

—Golf course architect Charles Blair Macdonald

Some golfers blast their ball from traps
With one adroit explosion,
But others, out in ten perhaps,
Depend upon erosion.

> —RICHARD ARMOUR, *Golf is a Four-Letter Word*

Unfortunately, the suit is so stiff, I can't do this with two hands, but I'm going to try a little sand-trap shot here.

> —ALAN SHEPARD, Apollo 14 commander and amateur golfer taking a golf shot on the moon

Social Graces
On the Links

Golfers don't fist fight. They cuss a lot. But they wouldn't punch anything or anybody. They might hurt their hands and have to change their grip.

—DAN JENKINS

Always throw clubs ahead of you; that way you don't waste energy going back to pick them up.

—TOMMY BOLT

No other group of professionals is self-ruled by an honor code in which players call penalties on themselves. Golf etiquette prevails. Can football etiquette or hockey etiquette be imagined? Golf has no Charles Barkley, who has spit at fans. It has no John McEnroe, the obscenity-shouter, nor does it have enforcers, late-hitters, or self-absorbed clods who moan that they aren't paid enough.

—COLMAN MCCARTHY

———— ·((·))· ————

A golf course is nothing but a pool room moved outdoors.

—FATHER FITZGIBBON (BARRY FITZGERALD),
after turning down an invitation to go golfing because of the profanity heard there, in *Going My Way*

———— ·((·))· ————

Thou shalt not use profanity; thou shalt not covet thy neighbor's putter; thou shalt not steal thy neighbor's ball; thou shalt not bear false witness in the final tally.

—GROUND RULES, Clergyman's Golf Tournament, Grand Rapids, Michigan

But since I cannot play at golf
Unless I swear a wee,
I'll give it up.
"What, golf?" they cried.
Nay, man—the ministry.

—19TH CENTURY SCOTTISH RHYME

If profanity had an influence on the flight of the ball, the game of golf would be played far better than it is.

—HORACE G. HUTCHINSON

Although I am smiling a lot, that doesn't mean my heart is smiling…the smile hides the real goal in the heart.

—SHIGEKI MARUYAMA

⸻

My style of play was aggressive, dynamic and mean.

—ALTHEA GIBSON, first African American member of the Ladies Professional Golf Association

⸻

I turn mean with a six-stroke lead. I'm not happy with a two-stroke win. I want to demoralize them.

—JOHNNY MILLER

⸻

Golf asks something of a man. It makes one loathe mediocrity. It seems to say, "If you are going to keep company with me, don't embarrass me."

—GARY PLAYER

⸻

Putting:
The Long and Short of It

Ninety percent of putts that are short don't go in.

—YOGI BERRA

Love and putting are mysteries for the philosopher to solve. Both subjects are beyond golfers.

—TOMMY ARMOUR

Real golfers don't cry when they line up their fourth putt.

—KAREN HURWITZ

When a putter is waiting his turn to hole-out a putt of one or two feet in length, on which the match hangs at the last hole, it is of vital importance that he say nothing. At this supreme moment he ought studiously to fill his mind with vacancy. He must not even allow himself the consolation of religion.

—SIR WALTER SIMPSON

———⚫———

I miss. I miss. I miss. I make.

—SEVERIANO BALLESTEROS' description of his four-putt at No. 16 at Augusta in 1988

———⚫———

Putts get real difficult the day they hand out the money.

—LEE TREVINO

———⚫———

To me, the scariest words in all of golf are, "It's a straight putt."

—BILL MURRAY

The first thing a television viewer realizes when watching a golf tournament is how the sport tends to make one inclined to whisper and avoid sudden movements, such as walking to the refrigerator during a possible birdie putt.

—PETER ALFANO

I am told that on the golf links he [Dwight D. Eisenhower] is better [with a putter] than he is with the long shots, and that doesn't surprise me.

—CHARLES DE GAULLE,
former President of France, in *Time*

Why am I using a new putter? Because the last one didn't float too well.

—CRAIG STADLER

Happiness is a long walk with a putter.

—GREG NORMAN

The Choke
Heimlich Can't Help

We all choke, and the man who says he doesn't choke is lying like hell. We all leak oil.

—LEE TREVINO

Suffering—! I've got a hen back home in Charlotte that can lay an egg farther than that!

—CLAYTON HEAFNER, on missing a three-inch putt and losing the Oakland Open by one stroke

That's Hoch as in choke, and you can print that, boys.

—SCOTT HOCH, after losing the
1995 Houston Open by one stroke

———— ((◊)) ————

A lot of guys who have never choked have never been in the position to do so.

—TOM WATSON

———— ((◊)) ————

Golf has humbled, humiliated, and just about licked every great athlete I ever knew who tried it.

—RED BLAIK, football coach

———— ((◊)) ————

I never prayed that I would make a putt. I prayed that I would react well if I missed.

—CHI CHI RODRIGUEZ

———— ((◊)) ————

On Par

Two things don't last long: Pros who putt for pars and dogs that chase cars.

—LEE TREVINO

If you keep shooting par at them, they all crack sooner or later.

—BOBBY JONES

Why does the prospect of hitting a golf ball nearly perfectly, again and again and again over the course of four hours, without gimmies and mulligans, in the wind, while others are watching, over greens the consistency of lumpy doughnuts, strike us as an achievable skill to master? Why do the rhythm and dexterity required to attain a sub-eighty round strike us as more learnable and achievable than sitting down and adroitly executing a composition by Bach?

—LEE EISENBERG, *Breaking 80:*
A Journey through the Nine Fairways of Hell

The Dreaded Bogey

These humiliations are the essence of the game.

—ALISTAIR COOKE

My reaction to anything that happens on the golf course is no reaction. There are no birdies or bogeys, no eagles or double bogeys. There are only numbers. If you can get that way, you can play this game.

—JIM COLBERT

I have found, in my own matches, that if you just keep throwing consistent, unvarying bogeys and double bogeys at your opponents, they will crack up sooner or later from the pressure.

—REX LARDNER

Ask yourself how many shots you would have saved if you always developed a strategy before you hit, always played within your capabilities, never lost your temper, and never got down on yourself.

—JACK NICKLAUS

Just reading the score card makes me so depressed. I mean, it's just no fun. But you have got to live with those days, too. When you win, that's what makes it so sweet.

—ANNIKA SORENSTAM, after bogeying three holes and ultimately losing a 2002 LPGA Tour match at Moon Valley Country Club to Rachel Teske

No matter what happens, never give up a hole...
In tossing in your cards after a bad beginning you
also undermine your whole game, because to quit
between tee and green is more habit-forming than
drinking a highball before breakfast.

—SAM SNEAD

———————

It took me seventeen years to get 3,000 hits in baseball. I did it in one afternoon on the golf course.

—Baseball legend HANK AARON

———————

Keeping Score,
or Why Golf Pencils Lack Erasers

The income tax has made liars out of more Americans than golf.

—Will Rogers

Golf is the hardest game in the world to play, and the easiest to cheat at.

—Dave Hill

For most amateurs, the best wood in the bag is the pencil.

—CHI CHI RODRIGUEZ

There is only one way to play the game. You might as well praise a man for not robbing a bank.

—BOBBY JONES, upon being praised for calling a penalty on himself when there were no witnesses to it

---

We have the cleanest professional sport of all. In baseball, if a guy traps the ball, he doesn't call it on himself, he tries to fool the umpire. We police ourselves. I've seen people call two-stroke penalties on themselves when it meant a $150,000 tournament.

—BRUCE CRAMPTON

Golf courses are the best place to observe ministers, but none of them are above cheating a bit.

—JOHN D. ROCKEFELLER, *A Rockefeller Family Portrait*

If I had my way, no man guilty of golf would be eligible to any office of trust under the United States.

–H. L. MENCKEN

When you walk off the golf course and you've won a golf tournament–you played by the rules, and did it right–only you know if you've behaved properly. Nobody else knows. So if you haven't done it right, it's a very shallow victory.

–JACK NICKLAUS

Winning

Victory goes to the player who makes the next-to-last mistake.

—Savielly Grigorievitch Tarakower

Victory is everything. You can spend the money, but you can never spend the memories.

—Ken Venturi

It's nice to have the opportunity to play for so much money, but it's nicer to win it.

—Patty Sheenan

They don't think I can win here, because I'm little and hit shorter. They think I get to the LPGA just to play—they think top 50, that's good [enough] for me. But I can win.

—Mi Hyun Kim, nicknamed "Peanut"

—————— ((◦)) ——————

The people who excel are those who are driven to show the world and prove to themselves just how good they are.

—Nancy Lopez

—————— ((◦)) ——————

Most golfers prepare for disaster. A good golfer prepares for success.

—Bob Toski

—————— ((◦)) ——————

If you break 100, watch your golf. If you break 80, watch your business.

—Joey Adams

—————— ((◦)) ——————

Losing

There are times when a golfer is tempted to throw her clubs away and forget the whole humblin' business. At other times, she wouldn't trade places with a queen—that's when the shots are long and true, and putts are dropping.

—BABE DIDRIKSON ZAHARIAS

You don't know what pressure is until you've played for five dollars a hole with only two in your pocket.

—LEE TREVINO

I hate to lose. But in golf, everybody loses because it is so hard mentally.

—TIGER WOODS

You hear that winning breeds winning. But no—winners are bred from losing. They learn that they don't like it.

—TOM WATSON

A lot more people beat me now.

—DWIGHT D. EISENHOWER, former U.S. President, on how his golf game had fared since he left the White House

The main idea in golf as in life, I guess, is to learn to accept what cannot be altered, and to keep on doing ones own reasoned and resolute best, whether the prospect be bleak or rosy.

—BOBBY JONES

I don't like doctors. They are like golfers. Every one has a different answer to your problem.

—SEVERIANO BALLESTEROS

———

I'm gambling that when we get into the next life, Saint Peter will look at us and ask, "Golfer?" And when we nod, he will step aside and say, "Go right in; you've suffered enough." One warning: If you do go in and the first thing you see is a par 3 surrounded by water, it ain't heaven.

—JIM MURRAY

———

Masters and Mastery

I'm not concerned about getting in the record books. A good obituary doesn't exactly excite me.

—JoAnne Carner

I never exaggerate. I just remember big.

—Chi Chi Rodriguez

I don't ever try to think of myself as the best player in the world, but I played like I was today.

—KARRIE WEBB, after winning the 1999 du Maurier Classic with her second consecutive 6-under-par 66

————— «(◎)» —————

Golf is a difficult game, but it's a little easier if you trust your instincts. It's too hard a game to try to play like someone else.

—NANCY LOPEZ

————— «(◎)» —————

The person I fear most in the last two rounds is myself.

—TOM WATSON, on the U.S. Open

————— «(◎)» —————

I'm the best. I just haven't played yet.

—MUHAMMAD ALI, prizefighter, on his golf game

————— «(◎)» —————

Golf is an open exhibition of overweening ambition, courage deflated by stupidity, skill soured by a whiff of arrogance.

—Alistair Cooke

—————

It's hard not to play golf that's up to Jack Nicklaus standards when you *are* Jack Nicklaus.

—Jack Nicklaus, on winning his 70th PGA tournament in 1984

—————

Because of them, I was able to play here. I was able to live my dream because of those guys. They came down and inspired me. I knew what I had to do. It really reinforced what I had to go out there and try to accomplish.

—Tiger Woods after winning his first Masters in 1999, about his guests Lee Elder and Charlie Stifford, who were among the first African American pro golfers to play in the Masters

—————

The Nineteenth Hole
and Other Consolations

Ah well. If we hit it perfect every day, everybody else would quit.

—LEE TREVINO, to Tom Watson

I would hope that understanding and reconciliation are not limited to the 19th hole alone.

—GERALD R. FORD, at the 1974 dedication of World Golf Hall of Fame

When I first came in I had sworn that I had never played a worse game—vowed that I couldn't hit a ball, that I'd have a bonfire of my clubs on the back green.... I was sick of the sight of them.... After sundry whiskies, hot, I began to think I had been playing quite a good game after all.

—J. McCullough, in his 1892 classic,
Golf in the Year 2000: Or, What We Are Coming To

—————◄◎►—————

If you foozle with your cleek,
And your putts are let's say—weak
If your drives, for all to see,
Do not always leave the tee
And to slice them is a habit—
If, in short, you're a rabbit.
Do not put your clubs away
Drink a Guinness every day.

—Guinness advertisement

—————◄◎►—————

If you drink, don't drive. Don't even putt.

—Dean Martin

Lifelong
Obsessions

The older I get, the longer my drives used to be.

—Chi Chi Rodriguez

I expect to play golf until I am 90—even longer if anybody figures out a way to swing a club from a rocking chair.

—Babe Didrikson Zaharias

How I would love to be 16 again. Then again, I would also love to be 58 again.

> —JoAnne Carner, LPGA Hall of Famer,
> when paired with a 16 year-old amateur golfer

If the sun is up, why aren't you playing golf?

> —Lee Trevino

My ideal in life is to read a lot, write a little, play plenty of golf and have nothing to worry about.

> —Arthur James Balfour, avid golf enthusiast
> and author of the Balfour Declaration,
> which touched off almost a century of
> intense conflict in the Middle East

He enjoys that perfect peace, that peace beyond all understanding, which comes at its maximum only to the man who has given up golf.

> —P. G. Wodehouse

The futeball and golfe be utterly cryed down and not be used.

—KING JAMES II OF SCOTLAND, banning soccer and golf in 1457 to induce Scots to take up archery for self-defense; the edict was rescinded in 1502, and the king took up the game himself

Some of us worship in churches, some in synagogues, some on golf courses.

—ADLAI STEVENSON

Golf is for smellin' heather and cut grass and walking fast across the countryside and feeling the wind and watching the sun go down and seein' your friends hit good shots and hittin' some yerself. It's love and feelin' the splendor o' this world.

—MICHAEL MURPHY, *Golf in the Kingdom*

If you don't succeed at first, don't despair. Remember, it takes time to learn to play golf; most players spend their entire lifetime finding out about the game before they give up.

—Stephen Baker

Go play golf. Go to the golf course. Hit the ball. Find the ball. Repeat until the ball is in the hole. Have fun. The end.

—Chuck Hogan